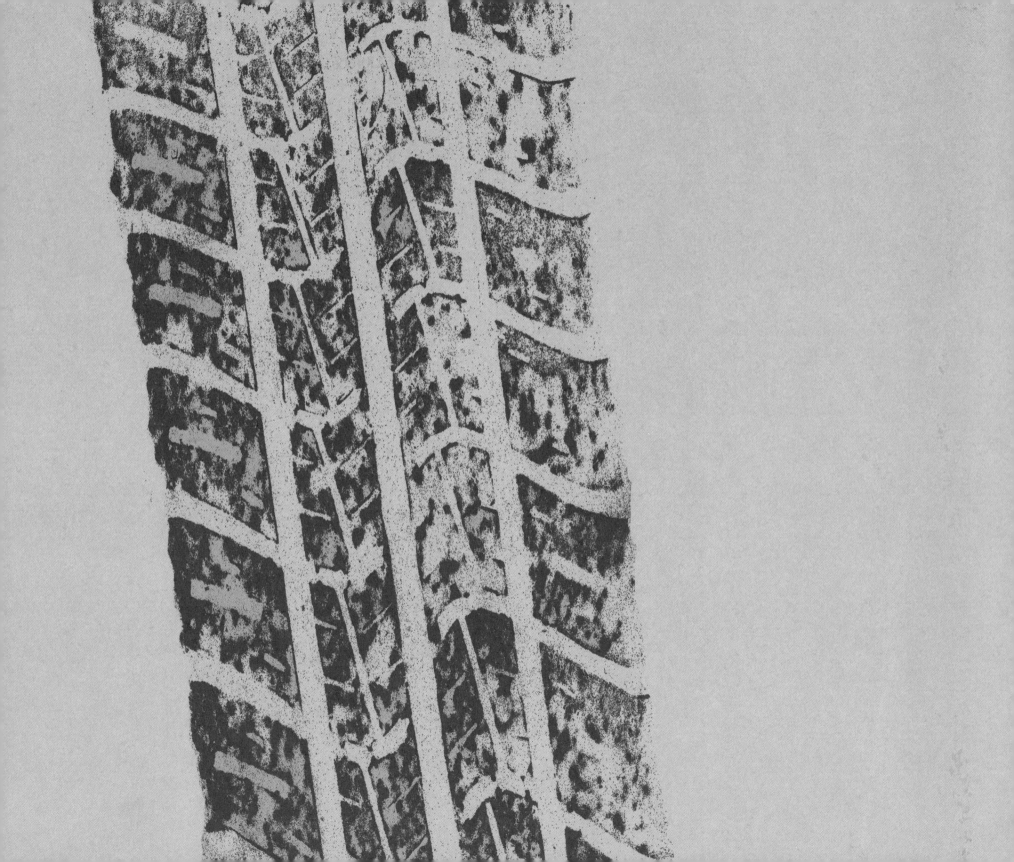

I DRIVE A BACKHOE

by **Sarah Bridges**
illustrated by **Amy Bailey Muehlenhardt**

PICTURE WINDOW BOOKS
Minneapolis, Minnesota

Working Wheels

Thanks to Bill Barnes of the City of Minneapolis
for all of the great stories. S.B.

Editor: Jill Kalz
Designer: Jaime Martens
Page Production: Tracy Kaehler,
Brandie Shoemaker, Zachary Trover
Creative Director: Keith Griffin
Editorial Director: Carol Jones
The illustrations in this book were created digitally.

Picture Window Books
5115 Excelsior Boulevard
Suite 232
Minneapolis, MN 55416
877-845-8392
www.picturewindowbooks.com

Printed in the United States of America.

Library of Congress Cataloging-in-Publication Data
Bridges, Sarah.
I drive a backhoe / by Sarah Bridges ; illustrated by Amy Bailey
Muehlenhardt.
p. cm. — (Working wheels)
Includes bibliographical references and index.
ISBN 1-4048-1604-6 (hardcover)
1. Backhoes—Juvenile literature. I. Muehlenhardt, Amy Bailey,
1974– II. Title. III. Series.
TA735.B746 2005
621.8'65—dc22
2005023793

Thanks to our advisers for their expertise, research, and advice:

Rod Sutton, Editor in Chief, and Walt Moore, Senior Editor
Construction Equipment Magazine, Oak Brook, Illinois

Susan Kesselring, M.A., Literacy Educator
Rosemount—Apple Valley—Eagan (Minnesota) School District

3

My name is Maura, and I drive a backhoe. My backhoe digs deep holes. It helps construction teams build roads and buildings. Some people call my kind of backhoe an excavator.

Different things can be attached to backhoes. Attachments may include augers, for drilling holes, or buckets that open and close like giant hands.

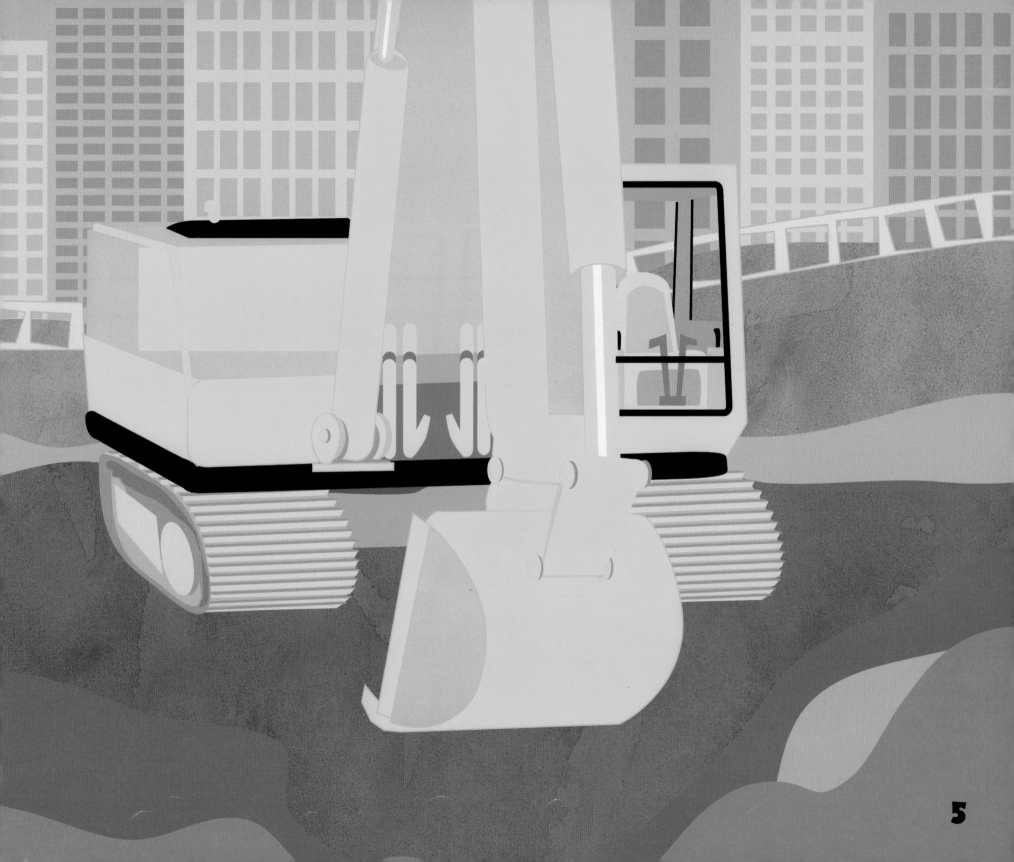

Before I start a job, I look under the hood. I make sure my backhoe has plenty of fluids.

I also check the tracks. If rocks or clumps of mud are stuck in the tracks, I scrape them out.

Backhoe operators also look underneath their vehicles. They check to see if the ground is wet. Puddles of liquid may mean something is leaking.

8

I hop into the cab and turn the key. My backhoe roars to life. The engine makes a loud, snarling sound. I let my machine warm up for a few minutes.

On cold winter days, backhoes must warm up. If they aren't warmed up, they won't run smoothly.

Before I dig, I need to know where underground pipes and cables lie. A city surveyor uses maps and measurements to show me where things are buried.

It is very dangerous to hit underground pipes. Leaking liquids may catch on fire, or poisonous gases may escape into the air.

When we find a pipe, I need to clear space around it before I can dig. I use a shovel to remove the dirt.

Many states have a law that says construction workers must clear a distance of 2 feet (60 centimeters) on either side of a pipe. This law helps make sure that pipes aren't hit or broken.

When I'm ready to dig,
I climb into the cab of my
warmed-up backhoe. Two
levers help me do the job. One
lever makes the big arm go up and
down. It also moves the bucket in and
out. The other level controls how the
bucket digs and swings the arm left
and right.

Different types of buckets have different jobs. Some open and shut like a clamshell.

My backhoe can dig through dirt, rock, or concrete. I scoop up a load, swing the arm around, and drop the load into a dump truck.

Backhoes are used when roads need to be dug up and rebuilt.

Sometimes, I find things in the ground as I dig. I may uncover bottles, tools, or parts of old buildings. Sometimes, I even find animal bones.

When backhoe operators uncover old
things, they call in special scientists called
archeologists who can tell them what they
have found.

Construction workers usually leave their big equipment outside overnight. That way, the machines are in the right place and ready for work the next morning.

At the end of the day, I lower the bucket to the ground. Then, I lock the cab. Now my backhoe and I are ready to rest for the night!

23

BACKHOE DIAGRAM

← — — arm

← — — cab

↗ tracks

← — — bucket

GLOSSARY

archeologist—a person who studies human life from long ago

auger—a metal attachment that looks like a giant corkscrew

bucket—the scoop on a backhoe or other digging machine

cab—the place where the driver of a backhoe sits

fluids—liquids in the engine that make it run smoothly

operator—a person who is in control of a vehicle or machine

surveyor—a person who tells construction workers where pipes are buried

tracks—metal belts that turn on wheels and make a backhoe move

FUN FACTS

Backhoes come in many sizes. Small ones may weigh 10,000 pounds (4,500 kilograms). Big ones may weigh up to 15 times more.

The work that backhoe operators do is usually noisy and hot. But many backhoe cabs are soundproof and air-conditioned to keep operators comfortable.

Sometimes, backhoe operators uncover dinosaur fossils. Fossils are the remains of plants or animals from long ago. In 1989, a worker in Virginia uncovered dinosaur footprints that were more than 200 million years old!

A backhoe loader is different than a plain backhoe. It looks like a tractor with a shovel on the front and a digging arm on the back. It has air-filled, knobby tires.

TO LEARN MORE

At the Library

Jones, Melanie Davis. *Big Machines*.
   New York: Children's Press, 2003.

Williams, Linda D. *Backhoes*. Mankato, Minn.:
   Capstone Press, 2005.

Zimmerman, Andrea, and David Clemesha.
   Dig! Orlando: Harcourt, 2004.

On the Web

FactHound offers a safe, fun way to find Internet sites related to this book. All of the sites on FactHound have been researched by our staff.

1. Visit *www.facthound.com*

2. Type in this special code for age-appropriate sites: 1404816046

3. Click on the FETCH IT button.

Your trusty FactHound will fetch the best sites for you!

INDEX

LOOK FOR ALL OF THE BOOKS IN THE WORKING WHEELS SERIES:

- I Drive a Backhoe
  1-4048-1604-6
- I Drive a Bulldozer
  1-4048-0613-X
- I Drive a Crane
  1-4048-1605-4
- I Drive a Dump Truck
  1-4048-0614-8
- I Drive a Fire Engine
  1-4048-1606-2
- I Drive a Freight Train
  1-4048-1607-0
- I Drive a Garbage Truck
  1-4048-0615-6
- I Drive an Ambulance
  1-4048-0618-0
- I Drive a Semitruck
  1-4048-0616-4
- I Drive a Snowplow
  1-4048-0617-2
- I Drive a Street Sweeper
  1-4048-1608-9
- I Drive a Tractor
  1-4048-1609-7

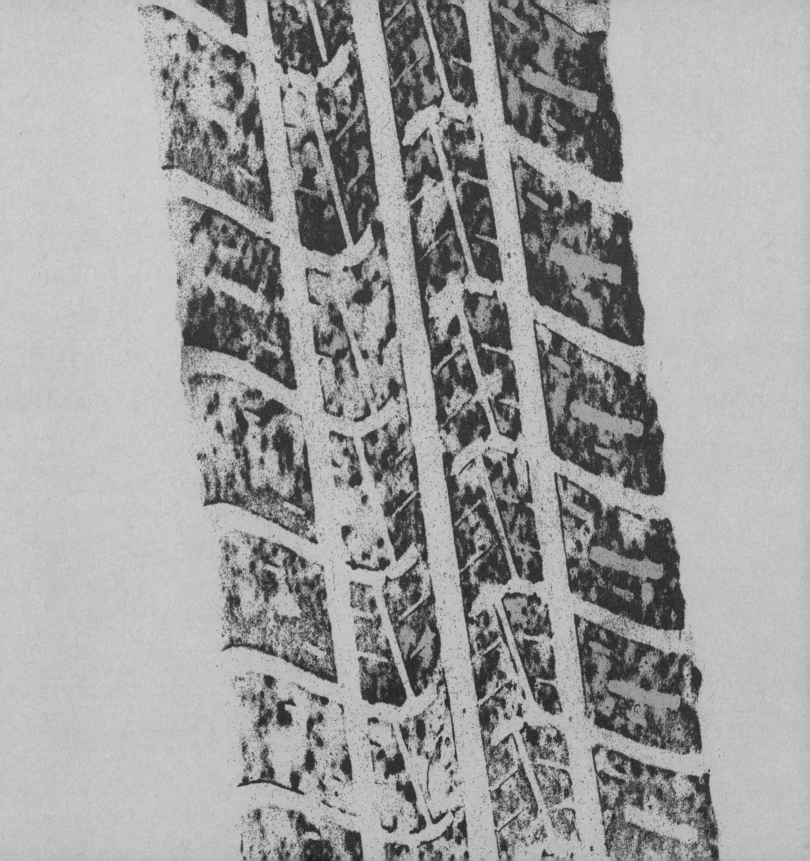